Which Animal Is That?

Cheryl Jakab and David Keystone

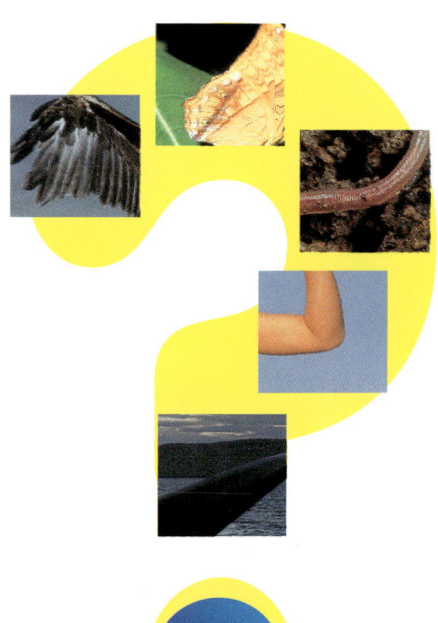

I have sharp claws called talons.
I have feathers.
I build my nest in high places.
I can see things from far away.
I can pick up small animals and carry them
with my strong legs and claws.

I can fly, walk, and hold things in my claws,
but I cannot swim underwater.
Can you guess my name?

I am an eagle.

I live in the sea.
I am the largest animal on earth.
I feed my young on milk.
I am warm-blooded.
I make sounds under the water.

I can swim in seawater, breathe air,
and leap out of the water,
but I cannot live on land.
Can you guess my name?

I am a whale.

I have three body parts:
a head, a thorax, and an abdomen.
I have six legs.
I have four beautiful wings.
I have two long antennae.
I feed on the nectar of flowers.
I lay my eggs on plants.

I can fly and walk,
but I cannot swim underwater.
Can you guess my name?

I am a butterfly.

I live in dark and damp soil.
I have a pointed head.
I have muscles that help me move.
I have tiny bristles on my body that grip the soil.
I help to make compost.
I eat my way through soil and make tunnels.

I can tunnel through soil and eat old plants,
but I cannot fly.
Can you guess my name?

I am an earthworm.

I have four limbs.
I have hair on my body.
I move around on my legs.
I have a skeleton inside my body.
I live on land.
I eat many different types of food.

I can walk, swim in water, and climb,
but I cannot fly.
Can you guess my name?

I am a person.

People are animals, too.